HOW TO DRAW DINOSAURS
AND OTHER
PREHISTORIC CREATURES

™

Mark Bergin

BOOK HOUSE

SALARIYA

Published in Great Britain in MMVII by
Book House, an imprint of
The Salariya Book Company Ltd
25 Marlborough Place, Brighton BN1 1UB

5 7 9 8 6 4

Please visit our website at **www.book-house.co.uk**
for **free** electronic versions of:
You Wouldn't Want to Be an Egyptian Mummy!
You Wouldn't Want to Be a Roman Gladiator!
Avoid Joining Shackleton's Polar Expedition!
Avoid Sailing on a 19th-Century Whaling Ship!

Author: Mark Bergin was born in Hastings, England, in 1961.
He studied at Eastbourne College of Art, and specialises in
historical reconstructions, aviation and maritime subjects. He
lives in Bexhill-on-Sea with his wife and three children.

Editors: Rob Walker, Stephen Haynes

PB ISBN: 978-1-905638-51-2

A CIP catalogue record for this book is
available from the British Library.

Printed and bound in China.
Printed on paper from
sustainable sources.
Reprinted in MMXIII.

**WARNING: Fixatives should be
used only under adult supervision.**

Contents

Making a start

Learning to draw is about looking and seeing. Keep practising, and get to know your subject. Use a sketchbook to make quick sketches. Start by doodling, and experiment with shapes and patterns. There are many ways to draw; this book shows one method. Visit art galleries, look at artists' drawings, see how friends draw, and, above all, find your own way.

Remember that practice makes perfect. If it looks wrong, start again. Keep working at it — the more you draw, the more you will learn.

Brachiosaurus

Parasaurolophus

Velociraptor

4

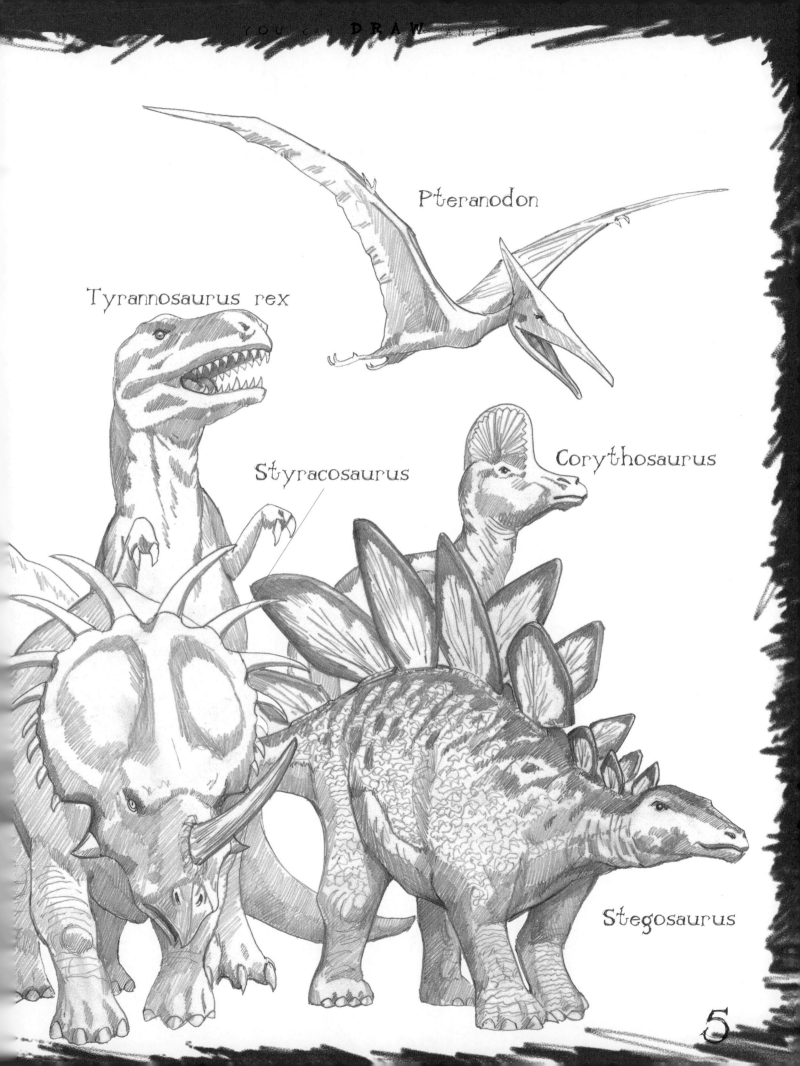

Pteranodon

Tyrannosaurus rex

Styracosaurus

Corythosaurus

Stegosaurus

5

Perspective

If you look at any object from different viewpoints, you will see that the part that is closest to you will look larger, and the part furthest away from you will look smaller. Drawing in perspective is a way of creating a feeling of space — of showing three dimensions on a flat surface.

Box construction lines can help with perspective.

The vanishing point (V.P.) is the place in a perspective drawing where parallel lines appear to meet. The position of the vanishing point depends on the viewer's eye level. Sometimes a low viewpoint can give your drawing added drama.

V.P.

6

Two-point perspective drawing

Low eye level
(view from below)

Two-point perspective uses
two vanishing points: one for
lines running along the figure,
and one on the opposite side
for lines running across the
figure. This gives a very
realistic three-dimensional
effect.

V.P.   V.P.

Normal eye level.

V.P.   V.P.

V.P.   V.P.

High eye level
(view from above)

V.P. = vanishing point

7

Materials

Try using different types of drawing papers and materials. Experiment with charcoal, wax crayons and pastels. All kinds of pens, from felt–tips to ballpoints, will make interesting marks. Try drawing with pen and ink on wet paper.

Ink silhouette

Remember, the best equipment and materials will not necessarily make the best drawing — practice will!

Hard pencils are greyer and soft pencils are blacker. Hard pencils are graded from 6H (the hardest) through 5H, 4H, 3H, 2H to H. **Soft pencils** are graded from B through 2B, 3B, 4B, 5B up to 6B (the softest).

Lines drawn in **ink** cannot be erased, so keep your ink drawings sketchy and less rigid. Don't worry about mistakes — these can be lost in the drawing as it develops.

Charcoal is very soft and is ideal for big, bold drawings. Spray charcoal drawings with fixative **(WARNING: ask an adult for help)** to prevent further smudging.

Wax crayons can be scraped away from parts of a drawing to create special effects.

Drawing pens can be used with a cross-hatching technique for tone.

Cross-hatching means lines that criss-cross one another to build up and develop tone gradually.

Pastels are even softer than charcoal, and come in a wide range of colours. Spray pastel drawings with fixative **(WARNING: ask an adult for help)** to prevent further smudging.

Felt-tips come in a range of line widths. The wider pens are good for filling in large areas of flat tone.

Sketching

You can't always rely on your memory, so look around and find real—life things that you want to draw. Using a sketchbook is one of the best ways to build up your drawing skills. Learn to observe objects: see how they move, how they are made and how they work. What you draw should be what you have seen. Since the Renaissance, artists have used sketchbooks to record their ideas and drawings.

Try drawing models of dinosaurs. It is good practice for your observation and understanding.

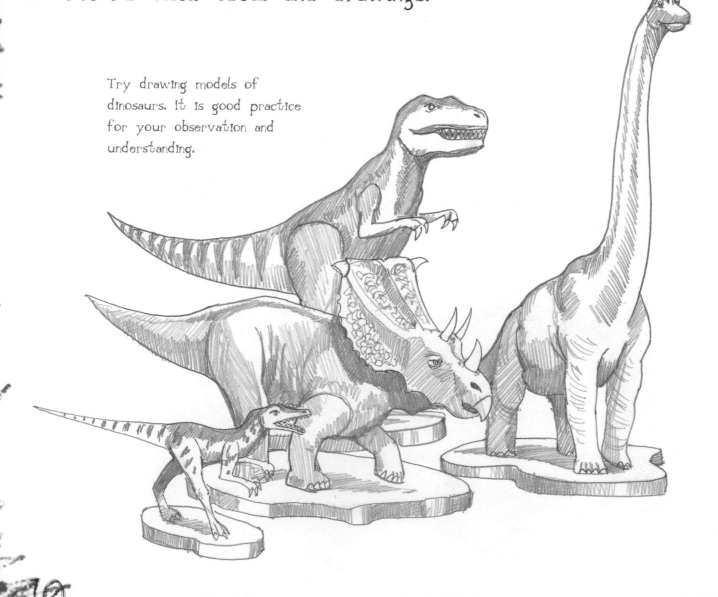

Museums often have life-size replicas of dinosaurs. They are usually happy for you to make sketches, as long as you don't use anything messy, like charcoal.

Replicas give a good idea of how a dinosaur looked.

A quick sketch can often be as informative as a careful drawing that has taken many hours.

Ankylosaurus
(AN-kill-o-sore-us or an-KYLE-o-sore-us)

This herbivore from the Cretaceous period was heavily armoured, which made it almost invulnerable to predators. The club-tipped tail was probably a dangerous weapon.

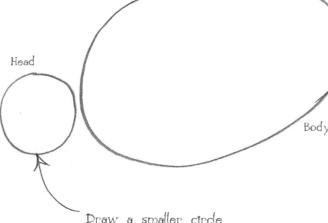

Draw one large oval for the body of the dinosaur.

Head

Body

Draw a smaller circle for the head.

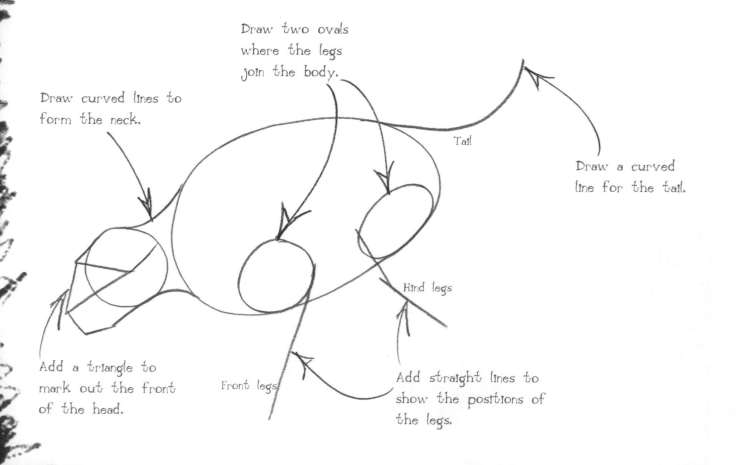

Draw two ovals where the legs join the body.

Draw curved lines to form the neck.

Tail

Draw a curved line for the tail.

Hind legs

Add a triangle to mark out the front of the head.

Front legs

Add straight lines to show the positions of the legs.

Draw a series of curved lines across the back of the dinosaur. These show the positions of the armour plates.

Add two curved lines to give the shape of the head.

Add two ovals for the club at the end of the tail.

Draw one long line along the centre of the main body to the end of the tail.

Draw in leg joints using circles.

Add tubes to the circular joints to make the legs.

Add detail to the club-tipped tail.

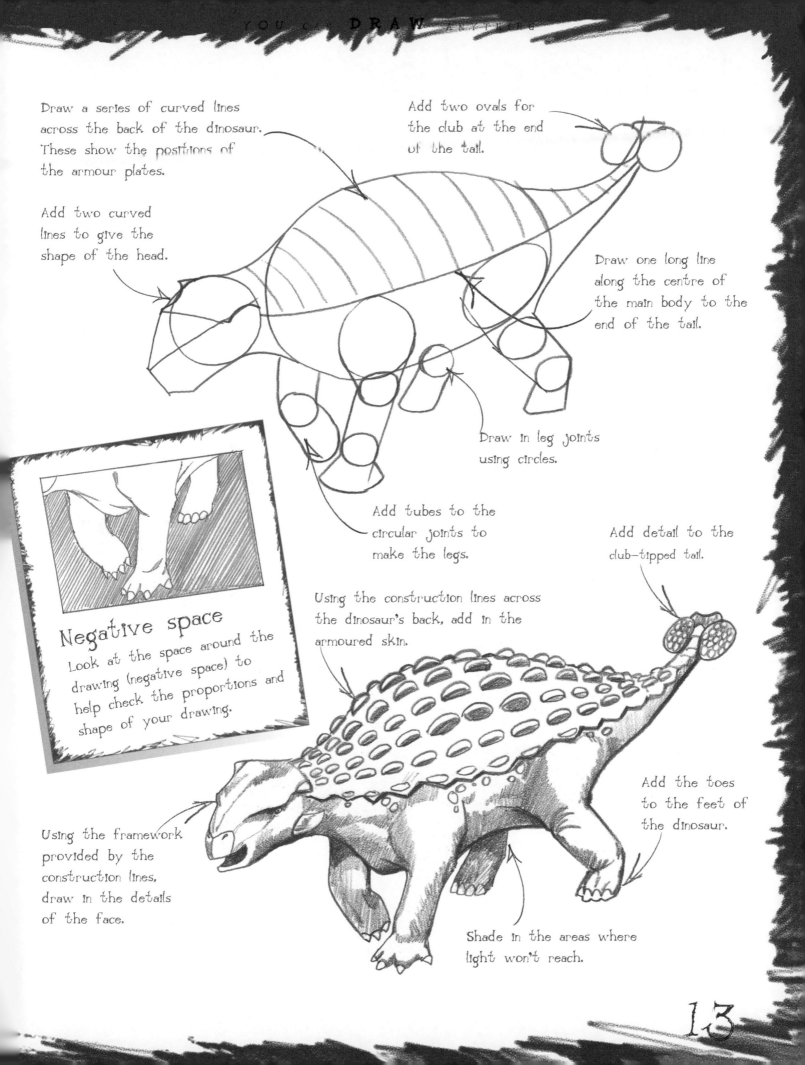

Negative space
Look at the space around the drawing (negative space) to help check the proportions and shape of your drawing.

Using the construction lines across the dinosaur's back, add in the armoured skin.

Add the toes to the feet of the dinosaur.

Using the framework provided by the construction lines, draw in the details of the face.

Shade in the areas where light won't reach.

13

Iguanodon

(ig—WAH—no—don)

Iguanodon was a herbivorous dinosaur that lived in herds and could grow up to 13 metres in length. Its footprints have been found in the rock layers of southern England, Germany and Spain.

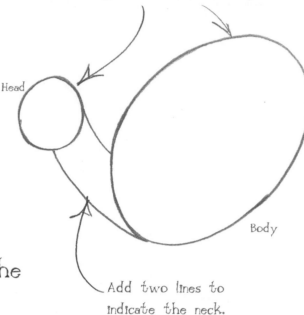

Draw a circle to form the head, and a larger oval for the body.

Head

Body

Add two lines to indicate the neck.

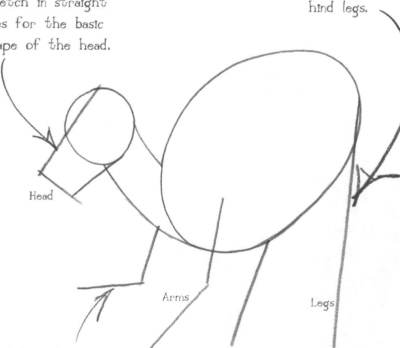

Sketch in straight lines for the basic shape of the head.

Head

Draw long, straight lines to indicate the hind legs.

Arms

Legs

Sketch in the position of the arms using straight lines.

Construction lines

Sketching in construction lines helps you create and keep the shape of your drawing. Once the drawing is finished, remove any that are left.

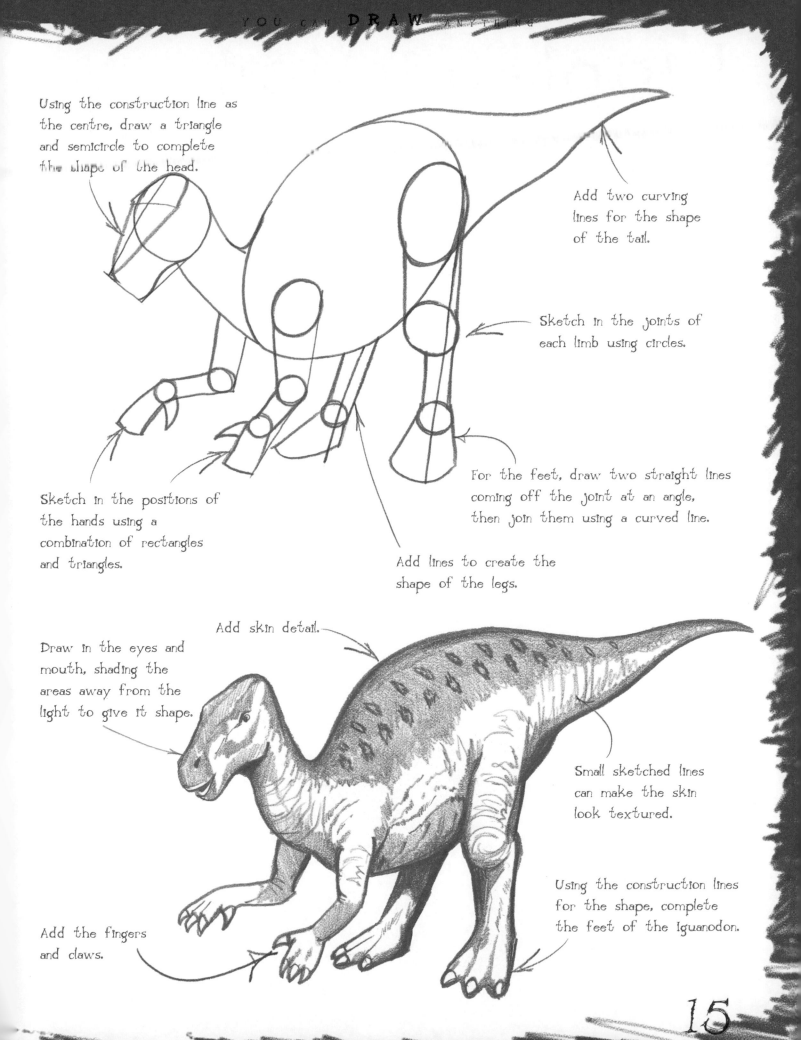

Using the construction line as the centre, draw a triangle and semicircle to complete the shape of the head.

Add two curving lines for the shape of the tail.

Sketch in the joints of each limb using circles.

Sketch in the positions of the hands using a combination of rectangles and triangles.

For the feet, draw two straight lines coming off the joint at an angle, then join them using a curved line.

Add lines to create the shape of the legs.

Add skin detail.

Draw in the eyes and mouth, shading the areas away from the light to give it shape.

Small sketched lines can make the skin look textured.

Add the fingers and claws.

Using the construction lines for the shape, complete the feet of the Iguanodon.

15

Liopleurodon

(lee-o-PLOO-ro-don)

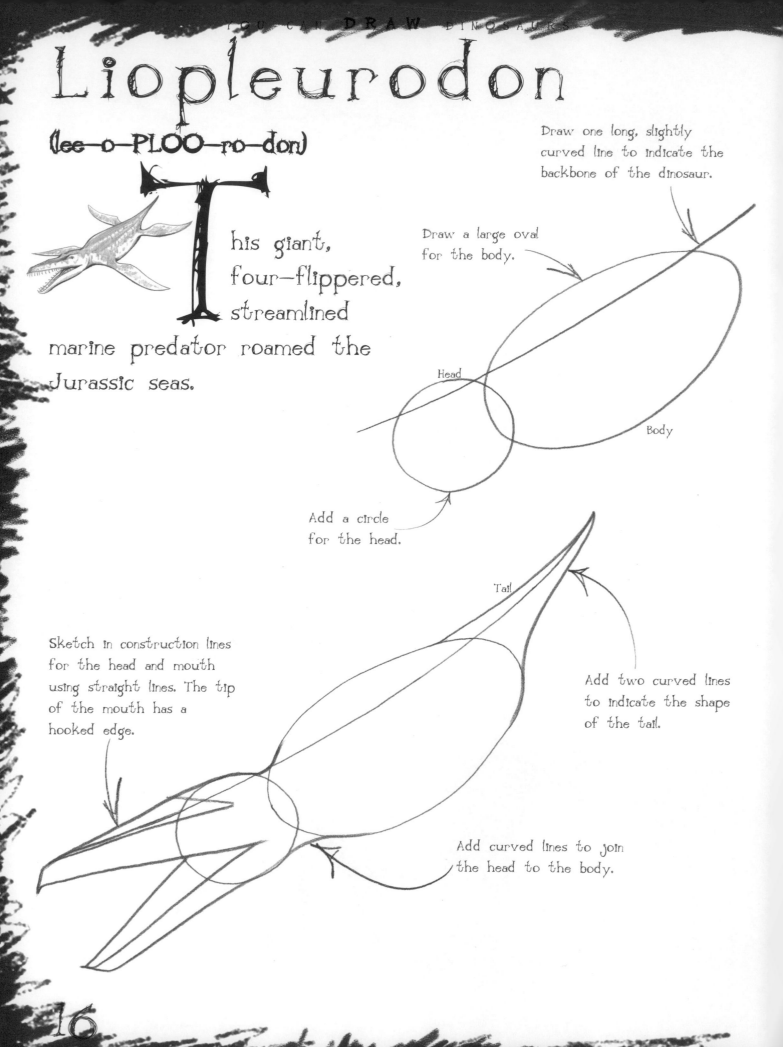

This giant, four-flippered, streamlined marine predator roamed the Jurassic seas.

Draw one long, slightly curved line to indicate the backbone of the dinosaur.

Draw a large oval for the body.

Head

Body

Add a circle for the head.

Sketch in construction lines for the head and mouth using straight lines. The tip of the mouth has a hooked edge.

Tail

Add two curved lines to indicate the shape of the tail.

Add curved lines to join the head to the body.

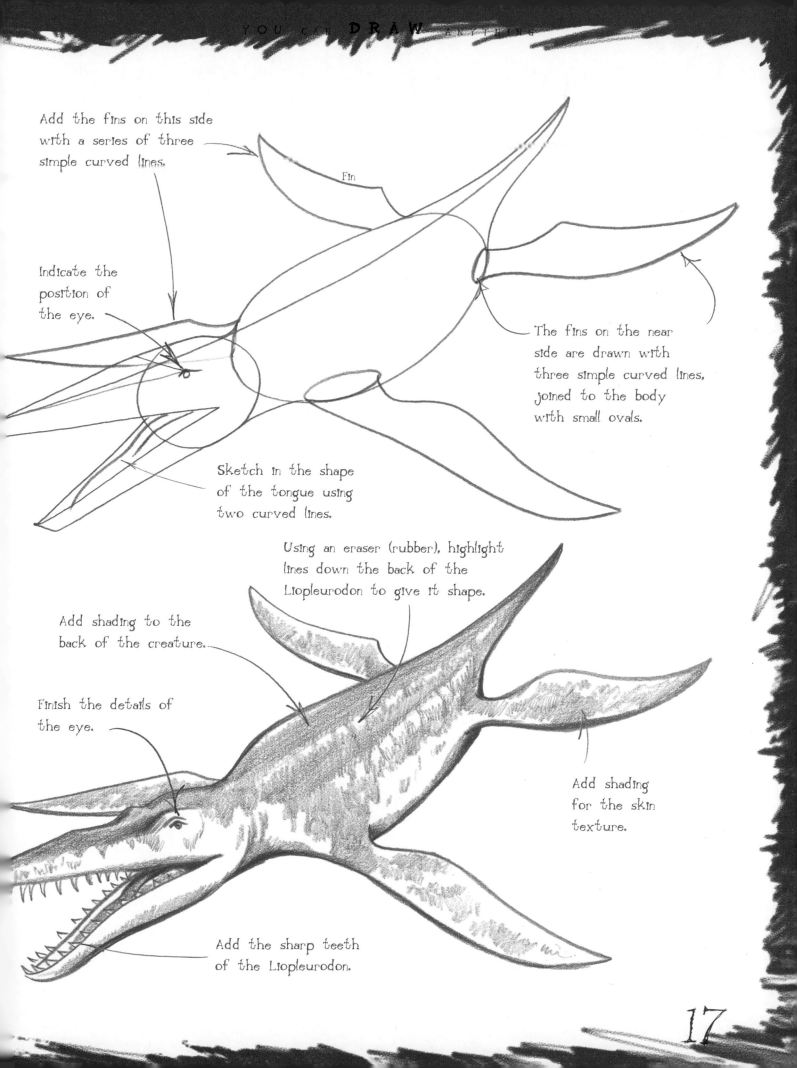

Add the fins on this side with a series of three simple curved lines.

Fin

Indicate the position of the eye.

The fins on the near side are drawn with three simple curved lines, joined to the body with small ovals.

Sketch in the shape of the tongue using two curved lines.

Using an eraser (rubber), highlight lines down the back of the Liopleurodon to give it shape.

Add shading to the back of the creature.

Finish the details of the eye.

Add shading for the skin texture.

Add the sharp teeth of the Liopleurodon.

17

Parasaurolophus
(para-saw-ROL-o-fus)

This was one of the 'duck-billed' dinosaurs. Its hollow, bony crest was longer than the rest of its skull, and may have been used to produce a foghorn-like sound.

Draw a circle for the head.

Head

Draw two large ovals for the main body.

Neck

Add two lines for the neck.

Join the ovals with two lines.

Sketch three straight lines to show the shape of the head.

Head

Draw a long, curved line to indicate the position of the tail.

Tail

Arms

Using a mirror
Hold your picture up to a mirror to look at it in reverse. This will really help you to see any mistakes.

The front arms are drawn with a series of small circles for the joints; join these with straight lines.

Legs

Sketch in the construction lines for the hind legs, using a series of straight lines with circles for the joints.

18

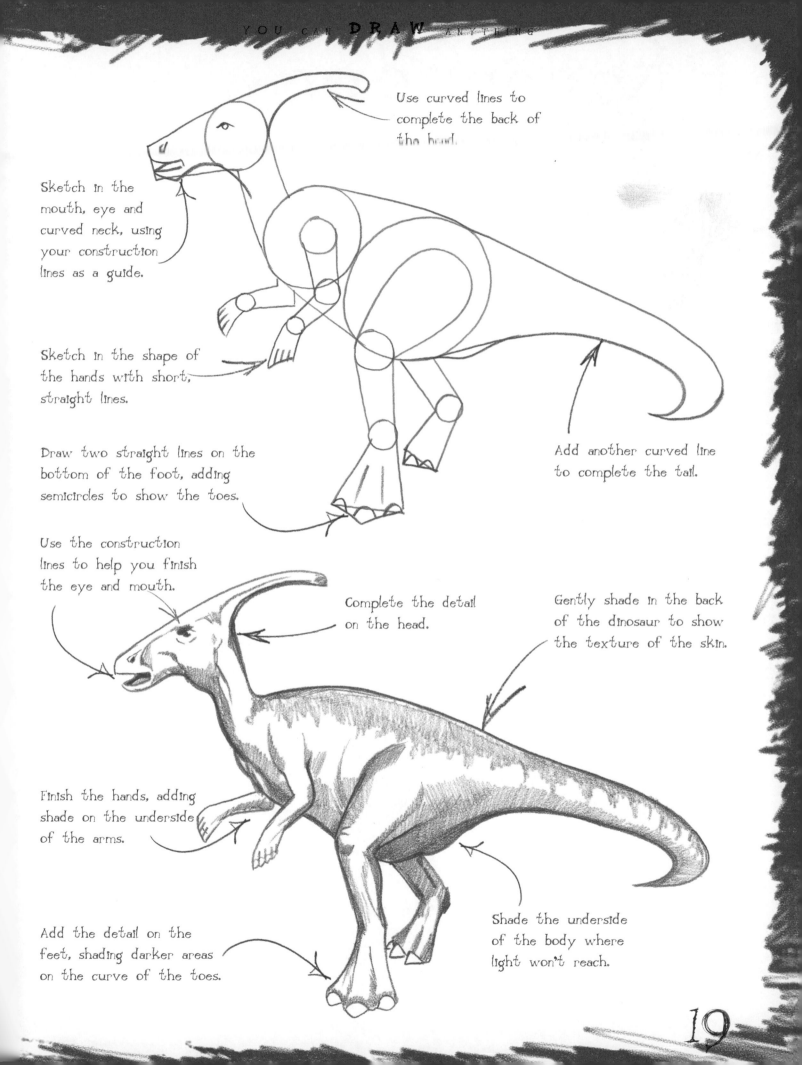

Use curved lines to complete the back of the head.

Sketch in the mouth, eye and curved neck, using your construction lines as a guide.

Sketch in the shape of the hands with short, straight lines.

Draw two straight lines on the bottom of the foot, adding semicircles to show the toes.

Add another curved line to complete the tail.

Use the construction lines to help you finish the eye and mouth.

Complete the detail on the head.

Gently shade in the back of the dinosaur to show the texture of the skin.

Finish the hands, adding shade on the underside of the arms.

Add the detail on the feet, shading darker areas on the curve of the toes.

Shade the underside of the body where light won't reach.

19

Pteranodon
(te-RAN-o-don)

The Pteranodon flew on huge wings of stretched skin. It was alive during the Cretaceous period. Its crest was presumably used for display.

First draw a simple cross.

Draw two circles for the head and body of the Pteranodon.

Head

Body

Sketch in the bottom half of the body using curved lines.

Sketch in the position of the head with three simple lines.

Draw a single curved line through the body of the Pteranodon for the arms.

Head

Arm

Wing

Leg

Add long, curved lines to show the top edge of the wings.

Sketch two curved lines coming down off the body of the Pteranodon to show the positions of the legs.

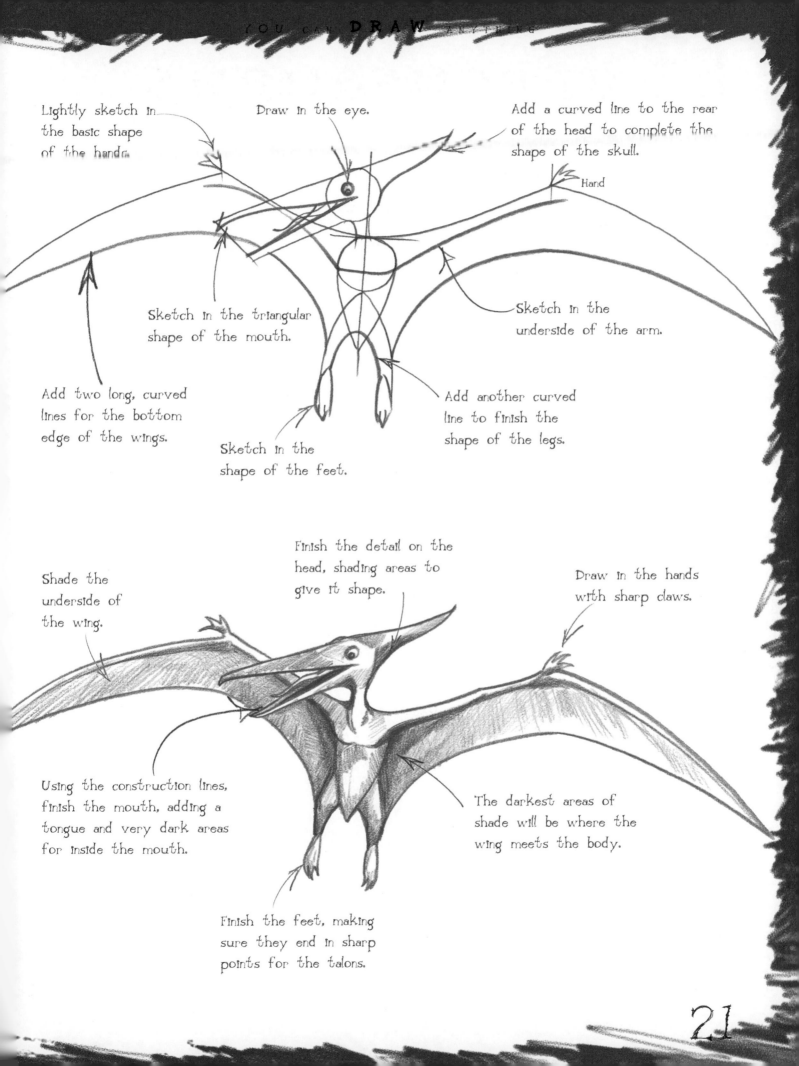

Lightly sketch in the basic shape of the hands.

Draw in the eye.

Add a curved line to the rear of the head to complete the shape of the skull.

Hand

Sketch in the triangular shape of the mouth.

Sketch in the underside of the arm.

Add two long, curved lines for the bottom edge of the wings.

Add another curved line to finish the shape of the legs.

Sketch in the shape of the feet.

Shade the underside of the wing.

Finish the detail on the head, shading areas to give it shape.

Draw in the hands with sharp claws.

Using the construction lines, finish the mouth, adding a tongue and very dark areas for inside the mouth.

The darkest areas of shade will be where the wing meets the body.

Finish the feet, making sure they end in sharp points for the talons.

21

Styracosaurus

(sty-RACK-o-sore-us)

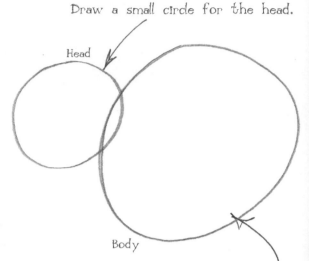

Draw a small circle for the head.

Head

Body

Draw a large circle for the body.

Styracosaurus ('spiked lizard') was alive during the Cretaceous period. It had up to nine horns and spikes around its neck to help it in fights, and weighed about 3 tonnes.

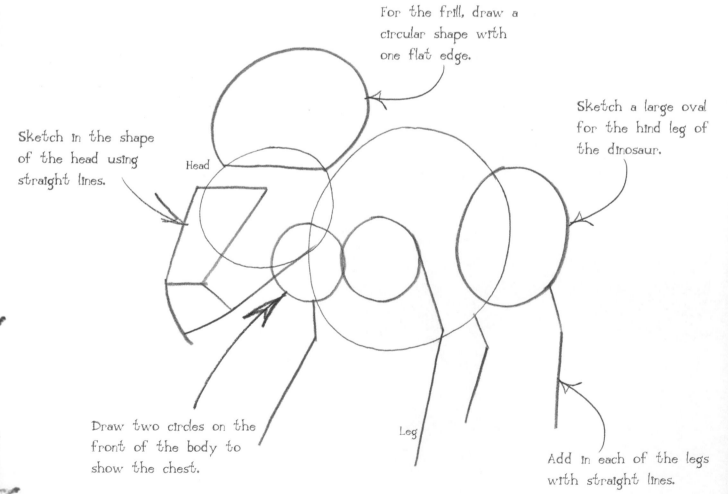

For the frill, draw a circular shape with one flat edge.

Sketch a large oval for the hind leg of the dinosaur.

Sketch in the shape of the head using straight lines.

Head

Draw two circles on the front of the body to show the chest.

Leg

Add in each of the legs with straight lines.

Draw one large horn on the animal's nose.

Using curved lines, add eight horns to the top of the head.

Draw a curved line down the back and along the tail.

Draw circles where the leg joints are.

Using the construction lines as a guide, add in the eyes and mouth.

Draw the lines for the legs, spreading outwards at the ends to form the feet.

Add more detail to the horns on the head.

Add a series of dots and some light shading for the skin.

Shade in the underside of the dinosaur for a three-dimensional effect.

Draw in the nostrils and add detail to the mouth and eyes.

Using shading and simple, light lines, give the dinosaur textured skin.

23

Stegosaurus
(steg-o-SORE-us)

Stegosaurus ('plated lizard') was a herbivore alive in the Jurassic period, 140 million years ago. It had large plates that ran down its spine from neck to tail. Its tail also had spikes on it for defence, that were nearly a metre long.

Sketch a large oval for the body.

Body

Head

Draw a small circle for the head and connect it to the body with curved lines to show the neck.

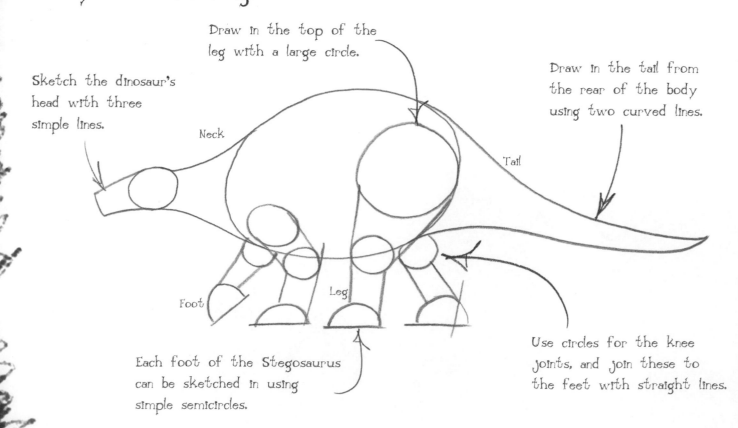

Draw in the top of the leg with a large circle.

Draw in the tail from the rear of the body using two curved lines.

Sketch the dinosaur's head with three simple lines.

Neck

Tail

Foot

Leg

Each foot of the Stegosaurus can be sketched in using simple semicircles.

Use circles for the knee joints, and join these to the feet with straight lines.

Draw two curved construction lines to help you draw in the plates on the dinosaur's back.

Each plate is drawn with four simple lines. Your curved construction lines (one for each row of plates) will help you judge how large they should be.

Sketch in the eyes and mouth.

Draw four straight lines coming out of the tail for the spikes.

Draw the second row of plates behind the first, again using the construction lines to judge their size.

Add detail to each plate with small lines and shading.

Shade the underside of the dinosaur to give a three-dimensional effect.

Finish drawing the eyes and mouth.

Finish the spikes on the tail by adding curved lines coming to a point at the end.

25

Brachiosaurus
(brack—ee—o—SORE—us)

One of the biggest Jurassic sauropods, the Brachiosaurus had a very long neck and could reach up to 27 metres in total length. Its giant bones have been found in eastern Africa and North America.

Head

Draw a small circle for the head.

Neck

For the neck, draw two long, curved lines connecting the head and body.

Body

Draw a large oval for the front of the body.

Head

Draw a smaller oval for the rear of the body.

Draw two overlapping ovals for the chest.

Draw a long, curved line down from the body to indicate the position of the tail.

Sketch in the legs using straight lines.

Tail

Leg

Composition

Using squares or rectangles to frame your drawing can make it look completely different.

Draw in the construction lines of the mouth, eye and top of the head.

Finish constructing the legs with straight lines.

Mark in the joints with circles.

Draw in the underside of the tail with a long, curved line similar to the top of the tail.

Sketch in the feet using semicircles.

Add the detail to the head, including teeth and shading to give it shape.

Use sketchy lines to give texture to the skin of the dinosaur.

Add shading, paying attention to where the joints are shown in your construction lines.

Shade in the areas where light would not reach.

Draw in the toes on each foot.

27

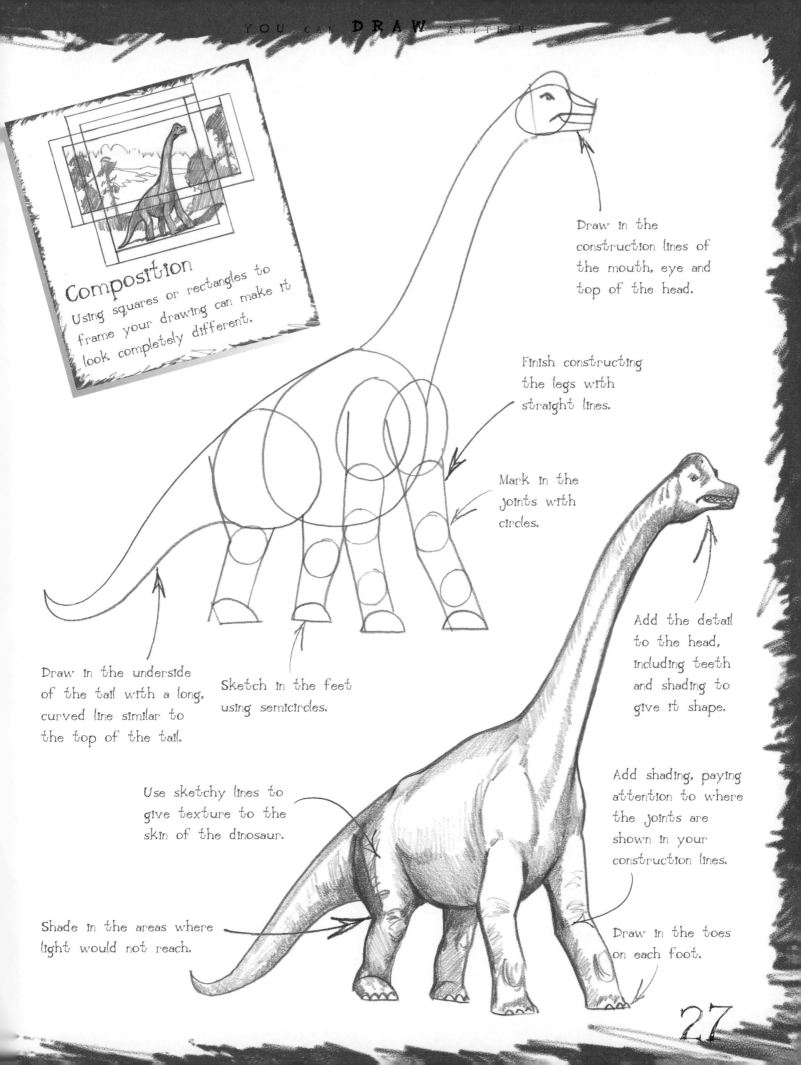

Velociraptor
(ve-LOSS-e-rap-tor)

The Velociraptor ('swift robber') lived 85 million years ago during the Cretaceous period. It was one of the fastest dinosaurs, moving at around 65 km/h!

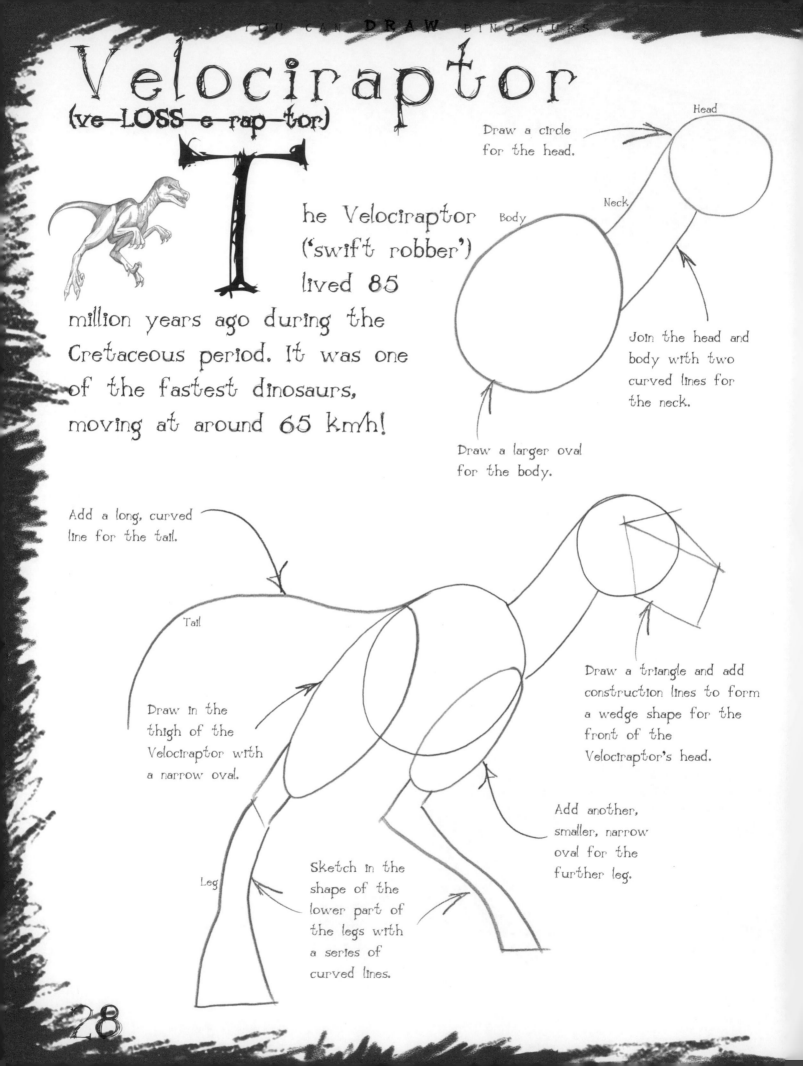

Draw a circle for the head.

Head

Neck

Body

Join the head and body with two curved lines for the neck.

Draw a larger oval for the body.

Add a long, curved line for the tail.

Tail

Draw in the thigh of the Velociraptor with a narrow oval.

Leg

Sketch in the shape of the lower part of the legs with a series of curved lines.

Draw a triangle and add construction lines to form a wedge shape for the front of the Velociraptor's head.

Add another, smaller, narrow oval for the further leg.

Add a long, curved line for the underside of the tail, continuing it to complete the underside of the body.

Use the wedge-shaped construction lines to sketch in the face.

Each arm is made up of three circular joints, joined up with simple lines.

Sketch in the shape of the toes.

Talon

Add talons to the ends of the toes.

Add shading along the back of the Velociraptor.

Use your oval construction lines to draw the shape of the thigh and leg.

Complete the head, drawing the detail of the eyes and adding teeth.

Using the construction lines, complete the hands, adding three talons to each.

Small lines can be added to give texture, such as wrinkles, to the skin.

Add shading and detail to the feet.

29

Tyrannosaurus rex
(tie-RAN-o-sore-us REX)

At 5 tonnes and 12 metres in length, Tyrannosaurus rex ('tyrant lizard king') was one of the biggest theropods of all time. It was alive 85 million years ago in the Cretaceous period. The massive jaws and teeth provided an awesome biting force.

Above the body, draw a circle for the head, and two lines to form the neck. The line for the rear of the neck should miss the head slightly, then curve in.

Head

Neck

Body

Draw a large oval for the body.

Sketch in the construction lines for the head.

Position the arms by drawing ovals for the chest and a circle for the beginning of each arm.

Draw in the tail using two curved lines joining at the tip.

Tail

Draw a line from the chest down to the legs to complete the body shape.

Draw a narrow oval for the top of the hind leg.

Legs

Sketch in the legs using straight lines.

Using the construction lines, draw in the main details of the head. Include the nostrils, mouth and teeth.

Use the construction line midway through the head to mark the top of the mouth.

Draw circles on the construction lines for the elbow and wrist, joining them with straight lines.

The hand is a basic shape consisting of four lines.

Add a circle for the lower joint of the knee.

Complete the detail on the head.

Use straight lines to complete the legs, with three pointed toes.

Use the construction lines to help you define the shape of the dinosaur's body.

Draw many lines on the dinosaur's skin to give it texture.

Add dark shading to the back for a chiaroscuro effect.

Chiaroscuro
The use of light and dark to create bold images is called chiaroscuro. Try this on your dinosaur to get more impact.

Finish the details of the feet, adding talons.

Glossary

Chiaroscuro The use of light and dark in a drawing.

Composition The positioning of a picture on the drawing paper.

Construction lines Guidelines used in the early stages of a drawing.

Cretaceous The period from 146 to 65 million years ago. Dinosaurs died out at the end of this period.

Fixative A type of resin used to spray over a finished drawing to prevent smudging. **It should only be used by an adult.**

Herbivore An animal that eats only plants.

Jurassic The period from 208 to 146 million years ago.

Light source The direction from which the light comes.

Predator An animal that kills and eats other animals.

Proportion The correct relationship of scale between parts of a drawing.

Reference Photographs or other images used to produce a drawing, if drawing from life is not possible.

Sauropods A family of dinosaurs with four strong legs and a long neck and tail. Sauropods include the largest dinosaurs of all.

Theropods A family of carnivorous (meat–eating) dinosaurs that walked on two legs.

Three–dimensional Having an effect of depth, so as to look lifelike or real.

Vanishing point The place in a perspective drawing where parallel lines appear to meet.

Index